D1737191

It's OK To Be The Boss

Knowing Your Job – Doing Your Job

Also by E. Perry Good

In Pursuit of Happiness
Knowing What You Want - Getting What You Need

published by New View Publications
P.O. Box 3021, Chapel Hill, NC 27515-3021

It's OK To Be The Boss
Knowing Your Job - Doing Your Job

by E. Perry Good

New View Publications
Chapel Hill, NC

Library of Congress Cataloging-in-Publication Data
88-060661
Good, E. Perry, 1943-
        It's OK To Be The Boss
        1. Management. 2. Supervision.
I. Title

ISBN 0-944337-01-5

Author Speaking Engagements
For information regarding speaking engagements by
E. Perry Good, contact the author at 510 Yorktown Drive,
Chapel Hill, N.C. 27516 or phone (919) 942-8491.

Quantity Purchases
Companies, professional groups, clubs, and other
organizations may qualify for special terms when ordering
quantities of this title. For information contact the Sales
Department, New View Publications, P.O. Box 3021,
Chapel Hill, N.C. 27515-3021.

Manufactured in the United States of America.

ACKNOWLEDGEMENTS

Many of the ideas about management and supervision in this booklet are based on Dr. William Glasser's Reality Therapy and Control Theory. I have worked with Dr. Glasser for many years and want to acknowledge his profound influence on my thinking. I would also like to acknowledge the contributions of Diane Gossen: the sections of Role Involvement and that on Complaints. These sections help solve two of the hardest problems in being the boss. I appreciate her encouragement and support. A special thanks to John Morganthau who taught me the Ideal Game when I was a young, desperate supervisor.

"The strongest principle of growth lies in human choice."

– George Eliot

TABLE OF CONTENTS

CHAPTER   **PAGE NUMBER**

I. IT'S O.K. TO BE THE BOSS

Most helping professionals become the boss because they are competent in something other than supervision. For example, I became a supervisor (or a "boss") because I was a competent counselor. I was not a competent supervisor. I was not trained to do supervision. I learned it while I did it, by trial and error. This booklet is designed to give you some simple tools that will allow you to be a more competent supervisor. It's O.K. to be the boss if you know what you are doing and what should be done. It's also easier and can even be fun.

What are some of the behaviors that a competent supervisor uses?

- assertive
- nips problems in the bud
- meets own needs
- helps others meet their needs
- creates a climate where people help each other
- consistent in giving orders/instructions
- good system of periodic employee checks to help them
- makes decisions with far reaching effects
- knows that one's "vision" makes a difference
- able to identify priorities
- not overwhelmed with work

When a supervisor doesn't think it's O.K. to be the boss, these are some of the symptoms:

- indecision
- lets problems build up, then blows up
- keeps too many secrets (for fear of imposing or interfering)
- tells too much (trying to get others to make decisions)
- martyrdom and paranoia
- swings from one extreme to the other (from too permissive to too dictatorial) when things go wrong
- doesn't give enough attention to employees (doesn't see this as one's responsibility as a leader)
- gives orders, then forgets them and gives contradictory ones
- ignores problems
- doesn't see the forest for the trees
- interrupts peoples' work with new things to do (doesn't let people finish what they were doing)

BECOMING A LEADER

1. In the process of leadership development, the first step is to make the decision to be a leader, or to be the boss.

2. The second step is to realize that there are leadership skills and they can be acquired with practice. However, all the training in the world in "techniques" and "theories" will not make a leader if the person does not have the gut feeling that s/he ought to be doing it.

3. The third step is to understand that decision-making is one of the main functions of a leader. Once the decision to be in charge, responsible, etc., has been made, this is only the beginning. From moment to moment, throughout the management process, the manager is constantly making decisions. S/he must be constantly sorting out what needs to be dealt with, what needs to be ignored, what needs to be passed on to others, what needs to be postponed for later action, and so on. Decision-making is a skill and improves with practice.

4. The fourth step is having confidence in yourself to be the leader. When a leader feels that "It's O.K. to be the boss" and carries this out in positive ways, there will be a regular flow of positive feedback that in turn will enhance the positive self-image of leadership.

LEADERSHIP STYLES

AUTOCRATIC - ACHIEVEMENT - DEMOCRATIC

Following the descriptions of each style is an opportunity for you to identify your own style.

AUTOCRATIC STYLE

- centralized leadership
- hires people who like structure
- tendency to get over-extended
- rarely asks for help or advice
- plans alone or on one-to-one
- rarely plans in groups
- makes decisions easily
- meetings are run by the leader, with little input from staff
- does not let workers make many decisions
- does not appreciate feedback
- remains personally detached
- maintains high personal standards
- wants to do more work in less time
- makes sure workers take the consequences

ACHIEVEMENT STYLE

- a combination of autocratic and democratic
- leader communicates "vision" to staff
- meetings have two-way communication between leader and staff
- acknowledges individual achievement
- includes staff in planning
- delegates some decision-making responsibility to appropriate staff members
- leader solicits and considers staff input and decisions reflect that
- involvement between staff members and leader

DEMOCRATIC STYLE

- participatory decision-making
- discusses politics and philosophy
- subject to dictatorship coups
- inclusive, informal
- standards are not always clear
- responsibility falls between the cracks
- plans everything several times
- meets frequently in groups
- meetings are leaderless
- sometimes lacks structure, consistency
- slow moving; everything decided by group
- active in promoting friendships, interaction

WHAT IS YOUR LEADERSHIP STYLE?

After reading the descriptions of each leadership style, mark on the line below where you think your leadership style fits between the two extremes.

Do not put yourself exactly in the middle.

AUTOCRATIC   DEMOCRATIC

Achievement style management is a combination of the autocratic style and democratic style. Each leader has a certain style that is more comfortable for her/him. The point of placing yourself on the continuum, and the reason for not putting yourself in the middle, is that it is helpful to decide where your honest leanings are. You will always be at least a shade more on one side than on the other. It may even vary according to the task to be done. Sometimes one style is appropriate, sometimes another. The point is to understand that there are the two extremes and to aim for a balance between the two.

II. PERSONAL INVOLVEMENT

A boss (or supervisor) must work to create an organization in which s/he and other employees can meet their basic needs. These powerful needs, as they are identified by Dr. William Glasser, are love or belonging, power, fun and freedom. They will be referred to often in this booklet. There is growing evidence in the literature on effective management that organizations that ignore employees' basic needs do not produce as well as those that provide a need-fulfilling environment. In other words, happy people do better work.

In order to create an environment which is need-fulfilling, balanced and achievement-oriented, two types of involvement must occur.

The first type of involvement is personal involvement. Personal involvement can be achieved in two ways: informally and formally by structured involvement activities.

The second type of involvement is role involvement, discussed in the next chapter. Role involvement is always present in any situation where there is a power differential (e.g., supervisor/staff member). It cannot be avoided in supervision because the staff member must deal with the supervisor to get some of his/her needs met. Staff members and supervisors interact to meet each other's needs.

A CHECKLIST OF SOME NATURAL INVOLVEMENT INDICATORS

Think about how many of these activities take place or are planned at work and how often they occur.

Socializing

- eat lunch together

- arrange dinners

- bowl, play softball, etc.

- improvise social events

- gather at parties after hours

- set coffee breaks with talk

- have birthday parties at work

- celebrate special holidays

Work Related

- help each other
- meet crises together
- thank people
- praise for achievements
- respond to peoples' needs
- organize retreats
- comment on co-workers' progress
- notice changes occurring

Style

- talk about personal life
- joke
- have fun
- hug, backrub
- sit beside someone
- look in peoples' eyes
- feel and show enthusiasm

Identity Building

- create a bulletin board with photos
- greet people by name
- ask someone how they are
- listen with care
- show people they are important
- give sincere compliments
- talk about TV, news, books
- sing together (group or band)
- create something together
- do arts/crafts
- care and show it

Attitude

- explore lots of options positively
- take risks—win some, lose some
- share information (healthy gossip)
- be honest
- show and promote trust

Personal Favors

- help, when needed
- lend or borrow money
- babysit
- share doctor and dentist names
- trade recipes
- give and get advice
- bring home-cooking to work
- give and get presents

SOME SYMPTOMS OF LOW INVOLVEMENT

Even if you think you are doing all the RIGHT things, some behaviors can take away from the good relations that do exist. Check off the things that happen in your office which erode good spirit and morale.

Negativity

- sarcasm

- making fun of peoples' weaknesses

- ridicule

- emphasizing why things won't work

- avoid giving praise

- complaining a lot

- making mountains out of molehills

- temper tantrums

Dishonesty

- lying
- cover-ups
- hiding grievances
- pretending you feel good when you don't
- preventing people meeting
- keeping people from comparing notes
- not doing what you said you would
- doing what you said you wouldn't

Lack of Trust

- assuming people will do it wrong
- avoiding joining in
- assuming people are accusing you
- being defensive
- getting mad before asking what happened
- waiting until everyone talks to say it

Other

- not talking about anything but work

- being rigid

- holding back praise

- not speaking to people (when angry)

- getting mad at one person, and taking it out on another

- taking credit for the accomplishments of others

- not accepting feedback (even when diplomatic)

The best way to reduce these symptoms of low involvement is: INCREASE INVOLVEMENT

NEW INVOLVEMENT METHODS

The need for involvement is universal because it is the chief way in which people meet the basic psychological needs common to everyone. Regular involvement activities are one way to help people meet their basic needs. A boss who is committed to running a need-fulfilling organization structures involvement activity into regular meetings. S/he does not see them as a waste of time. S/he sees them as the foundation of a cohesive organization.

Calling familiar involvement activities, such as birthday parties, "natural" involvement activities does not mean that new involvement methods are by contrast "unnatural." These new methods are slightly more structured than a casual conversation, but they are also very natural in the enthusiastic participation they generate. They also supplement very naturally the daily involvement that is part of any well managed organization.

Informal, natural involvement is almost never enough all by itself. When things are going well, there is a tendency for more human relations activities to occur. This will help things go even better. However, when things are going badly, the tendency is to drop the human relations and concentrate on the crisis. Yet this is the very time when involvement would help the organization to prevent or minimize the crisis. Regularity is needed to make involvement effective, to maximize productivity, and keep the symptoms of low involvement out of the organization.

One way to ensure regular application of involvement is to start *every* meeting with an involvement activity. This can be very short if necessary. (It can also be very long if desired or if more is needed.) Beginning meetings with involvement makes everyone feel acknowledged and included. We all need to be acknowledged by others to meet our needs. The involvement activity can focus attention and energy which is otherwise dispersed throughout the meeting in little side conversations and other digressions.

If you decide to start your meeting with a structured involvement activity, it is important to consider who will be the facilitator of these activities.

WHO SHOULD BE THE FACILITATOR OR GROUP LEADER?

It is possible for the person who is normally the meeting chairperson (the boss) to learn and perform the facilitator role, but it is often more effective if someone else does it. The group perceives the boss as a power figure *all* the time, regardless of the role being played in a meeting. A facilitator's role is much more effective when it is *neutral* from a power point of view. A neutral leader will minimize in the group any feelings of being manipulated or pushed or pulled in any way. Involvement activities work best when different people have the chance to be the facilitator.

Characteristics of a good facilitator include:

- a good listener

- chatty when appropriate

- able to follow instructions

- able to communicate well

- a sense of humor

- accepting of others

- enthusiastic

- curious

Pick staff members who have some of the characteristics above and who *want* to be the facilitator. Rotate this role—it is need-fulfilling to be the facilitator.

RULES FOR INVOLVEMENT ACTIVITIES

Make a photocopy of this page and post it on the wall where you hold your meetings.

1. Set up chairs in a circle, so everyone can see everyone else, with no tables in front of people.

2. The facilitator always goes first, as a model, and talks a lot.

3. One person talks at a time.

4. Do not interrupt.

5. Everyone looks at the person who's talking.

6. Everyone gets equal time.

7. Do not discuss or comment upon what a person says. Listen.

8. Under pressure, anyone can skip her/his turn. Group leader must remember to come back to anyone who skipped. Never force a person to participate, but don't encourage dropping out.

9. Each person should make an effort to participate positively as it will help both you and your group.

SEQUENCE OF INVOLVEMENT ACTIVITIES

When a group is having a number of human relations problems, or if the group has never met as a group before, it is strongly recommended to do all the involvement activities given here, in sequence, or do only the Success Involvement Activity. If meeting time is restricted, you can begin each of several meetings with one of the activities, starting with the Name Game, doing the Envelope Game (four questions each), and ending with the Good Things About You Game.

For the whole sequence, or the Success Involvement Activity, allow about one and a half hours. Make sure each group has not more than seven people in it, and not less than three. If your staff is larger than seven, divide into two or more groups.

The positive impact of the activities usually carries over to the meeting or workshop which follows, ensuring active participation and a successful outcome.

THE NAME GAME

Photocopy these instructions and give a copy to each group leader.

This is a good involvement activity for people who don't know each other. It also works well with people who do know each other well as it reveals people in a different way than usual. Talking about names is meaningful to everyone.

SET-UP: Minimum number of players is three; maximum is ten. If more than ten people are present, divide into sub-groups and select a leader for each. Ideal number of people per sub-group is five or six. Multiply the number of people per group by three or four minutes to get the total time it will take.

HOW TO PLAY:

1. Group leader goes first.

2. S/he simply talks about her/his name, using this list as a guide:
   What is your whole name?
   How did you get it?
   Were you named for someone?
   Do you like your name?
   Would you change your name?
   What would you change your name to?
   Have you ever had any nicknames?
   Do you know where your name comes from?

3. Group leader will talk about her/himself by answering these questions with anecdotes. The group leader's example will be followed by the others. S/he will talk from two to four minutes.

4. Group leader asks the next person to talk. If the person talks a lot, group leader lets them. If not, the leader should ask the questions in a conversational way, preferably not acting like it's a list you have to get through. Gently keep people on the subject.

5. Gently limit a person who is talking too long.

6. Limit discussion, but ask clarifying questions as needed. The purpose is to acknowledge each person in turn.

7. If two people talk to each other while a third is having a turn, hush the extra conversation nicely.

THE ENVELOPE GAME

Photocopy these instructions and give a copy to each group leader. This is a good involvement activity for any type of group.

SET-UP: Minimum number of players is three; maximum is ten. If more than ten people are present, divide into sub-groups and select a leader for each. Ideal number of people per sub-group is five or six. Multiply the number of people per group by three or four minutes to get the total time it will take.

HOW TO PLAY:

1. Photocopy questions for Envelope Game (see next page). Add your own questions first, if you wish. Cut the page into strips. Each question will be like a fortune cookie strip. (A variation is to spend five minutes at the beginning of the game making up questions. Give each person two strips of blank paper on which s/he must write a question. The two questions must be ones that the writer would be willing to answer her/himself.) Put all the questions into an envelope to prepare for the game.

2. Group leader goes first.

3. Group leader picks a strip from the envelope, answers the question *fully*, talking for about two minutes. This will provide a model for others.

4. Group leader passes the envelope to next person, asks her/him to pick a slip and talk about it. If the person doesn't talk enough, here are some things the group leader can say to encourage more talk:

> What happened then?
> Did you like it?
> Do you still think so?
> Was it fun?

After the person has finished, ask her/him to pick a second question and talk about it.

5. Group leader passes envelope to next person, and so on. If a person doesn't like a question, s/he can have *one* substitution.

6. Same rules for listening, etc., as in the Name Game (page 21).

7. After everyone has had a turn, the game may end or the group leader may take another turn, facilitate everyone taking another turn, and so on. In this way, up to four questions may be answered during the activity. The greater the need for involvement, the more turns should be taken.

QUESTIONS FOR THE ENVELOPE

Make photocopies of these pages. Cut questions into strips, one question per strip. Fold strips and put them in an envelope. Game organizer or players can make up more questions, if desired.

What makes you happy?

What makes you angry?

If you could have one wish, what would it be?

What qualities do you look for in a friend?

What would you do with a million dollars?

What's something you're proud of?

How do you judge how smart a person is?

What is the most important thing in your life?

What means more to you than anything else?

What is the most beautiful thing you've ever seen?

What do people like in you the most?

What *one* thing about yourself would you *not* change and why?

When do you feel best?

What one day in your life did you enjoy the most?

What were you afraid to do but did anyway?

When did you need help and ask for it?

What was a difficult decision you made?

When did you help someone to do something he or she couldn't do?

What do you like about being different?

What do you especially like to do?

What is a joyful experience you have had?

What is a decision you made that changed your life?

What is a successful experience you have had?

What would you do with $1,000 without giving any of it away?

THE GOOD THINGS ABOUT YOU GAME

Make a photocopy of these instructions and give it to each group leader. This game is for people who have known each other for some time *or* who have just met but who have already played the Name Game and the Envelope Game.

SET-UP: Minimum number of players is three; maximum is ten. If more than ten people are present, divide into sub-groups and select a leader for each. Ideal number of people per sub-group is five or six. Multiply the number of people per group by two minutes to get the total time it will take.

HOW TO PLAY:

1. Group leader starts by addressing another person *by name* and says, "Clarence, two good things I noticed about you are...." Some examples may be, "your way of helping people and your efficiency," *not* superficial things like "your red sweater and you're nice."

2. Group leader turns to another person and says, "Jane, it's your turn to say two good things you noticed about Clarence. Start with his name, please."

3. Group leader turns to another person and says, "Sam, it's your turn to say two good things you noticed about Clarence."

4. After everyone has addressed Clarence, group leader turns to next person: "Jane, two good things I noticed about you...", and asks everyone in the group, in turn, to address Jane.

5. After everyone has addressed Jane, group leader will address Sam and ask everyone, in turn, to address Sam, and so on until everyone in the group has been addressed in this way by everyone else.

6. By the end of the game, everyone in the group will have heard two good qualities about her/himself said by everyone in the group. This is a form of "positive bombardment" which is often needed and useful. (NOTE: The group leader should not forget her/his own turn to hear good things about her/himself, although this should not come first. It can come in the middle or last.)

SUCCESS INVOLVEMENT ACTIVITY

NOTE TO LEADERS: It is crucial in the first two parts of this exercise that the leader go first and serve as a model by talking *a lot.*

The Name Game

- What is your whole name?
- Would you like to change your name?
- How did you get it?
- What would you change it to?
- Were you named for someone?
- Do you have any nicknames?
- Do you like your name?
- Have you ever had any nicknames?

Questions

1. Tell us something you would especially like to do.
2. Tell us about a joyful experience you have had.
3. Tell us about a decision you have made that has affected your life.
4. Tell us about a successful experience that you have had.

Cards

Pass out to each member of your group a 5 x 7 index card and a sheet of self-adhesive labels. (Each person needs enough labels to have one for everyone else in the group, and the labels need to be small enough so one from every person in the group will fit on one 5 x 7 card.) Instruct the group members to write their name on the index card. On the labels (one for each group member) they are to write one or two positive qualities they have observed in the group member. Then, have each person pass around her/his index card, and the group members, in turn, attach the label for the person whose name is on the card and read out loud the positive qualities they have written on the label. *Be sure that you do this for each individual, so that all members of the group are listening to what is being said about every other member.*

After the group has finished, you can ask whether anyone had anything on their card that was surprising or that they want to ask questions about, but don't stop the group for this—do it at the end.

OTHER INVOLVEMENT ACTIVITIES

Good, five-minute involvement activities for the beginning of staff, committee, or board meetings are so-called "sentence stumps." You make up the beginning of a sentence and each person, in turn (starting with the group leader), finishes the sentence. Here are some sentence stumps to use:

The best thing that happened to me this week was ....

I'm proud of .... (can be personal or work-related)

This week I learned ....

I accomplished .... (today, this week, this month, or anytime)

I wish .... (this can be a good start for a planning session)

This game can have as many people in the group as you wish. You can make up your own sentence stumps, but make sure they are *positive.*

PROBLEMS WITH INVOLVEMENT ACTIVITIES

"Involvement activities take too much time."
"Involvement activities are stupid." "Involvement activities
have nothing to do with our business." "Involvement
activities are a waste of time." Etc.

People with these attitudes do not understand that
involvement is the fuel that keeps everything going in the
organization. A person who continues to avoid involvement
may want to avoid human contact for her/his own reasons.
Symptoms may include being late to meetings, missing
meetings, snickering and making fun of the activity, making
smart-aleck answers in the involvement games, etc. S/he
hopes the negative behavior will cause the involvement
activities to stop.

WHAT TO DO ABOUT IT

Involvement activities can be done in a short amount of
time. Convince a resistant person to participate actively and
positively in several short involvement activities. After the
agreed-upon number of meetings, discuss with *the group*
whether or not to continue. By then, the group will
probably think it is worthwhile having involvement
activities.

If the group decides to continue the activities but the
resistant individual resumes negative behaviors, it is up to
the supervisor to speak to the person individually and
explain that these activities will continue to be part of the
meetings and, consequently, are part of the job if the
individual chooses to remain in the organization.

INVOLVEMENT LEADS TO COMMITMENT

It would be a good idea to make a poster with the above sentence on it and put it up in your meeting place. Many of the management problems experienced by organizations would evaporate if there were an increase in both natural socializing and more formal involvement activities.

Involvement helps people meet their basic needs in the following ways:

- Involvement helps to recognize achievement.

- Involvement provides pleasurable interaction.

- Involvement helps to create a sense of belonging.

- Involvement builds a positive self-image which enhances freedom of choice.

When involvement helps people to meet their needs in the workplace, good work is the result.

HELPFUL BOOKS ON INVOLVEMENT

(SOURCES FOR MORE INVOLVEMENT ACTIVITIES)

VALUES CLARIFICATION: A Handbook of Practical Strategies for Teachers and Students by Sidney B. Simon, Leland W. Howe and Howard Kirschenbaum, and *100 WAYS TO ENHANCE SELF CONCEPT IN THE CLASSROOM* by Jack Canfield and Harold C. Wells. Although the activities in these books are designed for children, over 80% of them are ideal for adults as well.

TRIBES: A Human Development Process for Educational Systems by Jeanne Gibbs and Andre Allen. This book gives you many involvement activities suitable for adults, and it gives you more of the rationale for involvement. It can be ordered from Center Source Publications, P.O. Box 436, Santa Rosa, CA 95402.

THE NEW GAMES BOOK, published by Dolphin Books, Garden City, NY. For those who prefer physical games to verbal games, this book is an excellent source. The games are non-competitive and fun. It is illustrated with photographs.

III. ROLE INVOLVEMENT

A good supervisor clearly understands that s/he has role power which goes far beyond her/his personal power. In the performance of her/his duties s/he will be required to use authority to exert control over others and to deal with matters s/he may, as an individual, not even choose to address. The use of role involvement in a discipline situation engages the person being disciplined more at the thinking level than at the emotional level. Therefore, it is more likely that s/he can objectively evaluate her/his behavior rather than become emotional or angry. The use of role involvement protects the good personal involvement which has been carefully built up.

Role involvement is basically one's job description. Any statement that begins with "My job is...," or "The policy is...," or "The expectation is...," or "My role is...," or "Your task is...," etc., describes role involvement. This role involvement is the appropriate starting point when one is explaining program expectations or enforcing rules.

An "I need" statement by the supervisor clarifies what s/he wants rather than what s/he doesn't want. A "don't want" can too often be perceived as criticism, whereas statements such as, "I need your reports in order to make budget projections," or "I need to know what your plan is for coverage during shift change," or "I need you to come to me if you want policy clarification," clearly focus the discussion at a professional level toward positive change. This is more productive than focusing on past mistakes which tends to leave the person with less sense of control and with bad feelings.

Role definition is a vital part of good management because it outlines both the powers and responsibilities for each position. An effective supervisor leads her/his staff through an exercise which delineates staff responsibilities with regard to clients, students, or customers, as well as the management's role with regard to staff. An effective format to use for this purpose is the following grid:

MY JOB IS	YOUR JOB IS
MY JOB IS NOT	YOUR JOB IS NOT

The supervisor presents this grid as a guideline for brainstorming. For example, in a residential rehabilitation facility the grid might read as follows:

STAFF	CLIENT
MY JOB IS	**YOUR JOB IS**
• to supervise • to evaluate • to enforce • to recommend • to report • to encourage	• to follow the rules • to participate in the program • to get along with the group • to do assigned chores • to make decisions yourself • to keep clean
MY JOB IS NOT	**YOUR JOB IS NOT**
• to cover up • to lend money • to take abuse	• to do my job • to decide for another • to make policy

etc.

On the other hand, for a classroom teacher brainstorming with a group of students, the grid might look like this:

TEACHER	STUDENT
MY JOB IS	**YOUR JOB IS**
• to present information • to evaluate • to encourage • to answer questions • to enforce policy	• to learn • to ask questions • to ask for help • to demonstrate what you've learned • to conduct yourself so as not to prevent others learning
MY JOB IS NOT	**YOUR JOB IS NOT**
• to learn for you • to make you learn • to take abuse	• to do my job • to decide for her/him • to discipline other students

A second use of this grid is for the supervisor to engage in the same process with regard to her/his role in supervising staff. After all, the job of a supervisor is basically to see that everyone else does her/his job. Such a grid might look like this:

SUPERVISOR	STAFF
MY JOB IS	**YOUR JOB IS**
• to supervise • to evaluate • to make decisions • to regulate • to plan	• to perform duties • to contribute ideas • to ask questions • to make recommendations • to co-operate with team • to implement program • to enforce rules
MY JOB IS NOT	**YOUR JOB IS NOT**
• to do your job • to cover up • to take abuse	• to do her/his job • to single handedly change the system • to take abuse

These exercises will each take a couple hours. (Subgroups may be used initially to bring forth ideas.) Some teams I have worked with that were involved in new programs have taken several sessions to hash these out to reach a consensus. For the effective operation of any organization, it is crucial for all staff to have the same picture of program goals, policies, and their respective roles.

A final part of this exercise involves role playing whereby groups of four or five people prepare a candidate to be interviewed by receivers of service with regard to their role. Encourage those role-playing the receivers of service to aggressively search for loop holes and to challenge policies. The job of the staff candidate is to remain emotionally objective and to clarify policy and choices. Encourage the use of role-defining words such as "the

38

program," "the policy," "the rule," "the expectation," and "from my experience." Also, carefully monitor the language used depending on the receivers of service. For example, a corrections worker might say to an inmate going on a temporary absence from the prison, "It's your responsibility to keep the peace and come back clean. It's my job to search you on your return and if you're carrying any contraband, then you will be charged." An elementary school principal might say to an aggressive student, "This is a place where students can feel safe. If you keep hurting other people I'll be in a position where I have to suspend you from our program. I don't want to do that. I would prefer that together we figure out a way for you to make some friends and feel more comfortable here." A supervisor in a child care facility might say to a staff member, "Generally, things have been going well in the program. There seems to be a small problem that arose on last night's shift and it's my job to talk to you and help you evaluate how you handled it and to figure out what to do if this arises again." Such clarification of intent and expectations can direct a person towards better behavior. There is no need to find fault or to defend. Excuses are received without debate. Change is the goal. The use of role involvement is the key to both conflict resolution and effective discipline.

IV. SUPERVISION

Even if you are not the overall "boss" of an organization, you may be the supervisor of a group within the organization. For this group, you are in effect "the boss." Being a "boss" and being a supervisor require essentially the same skills, no matter at what organizational level you may be working. It's O.K. to be a supervisor if you understand clearly what a supervisor needs to do.

WHAT A SUCCESSFUL SUPERVISOR DOES

The main purposes of supervision are:

- Communication

- Support

- Evaluation

- Problem Solving

The supervisor is a facilitator who promotes the growth of those whom s/he is supervising. As a result, the quality and quantity of work increases. The worker's success is a need-fulfilling activity which further encourages personal growth. This positive process is encouraged and stimulated by the supervisor.

IS "SUPERVISOR" A DIRTY WORD?

Here are some images which people often associate with being a supervisor. Check yourself and see if you agree that a supervisor is:

- bossy

- always looking over your shoulder

- picky

- someone who does not care about *you*, only about the *work* getting done

- only found in large corporations

- a "cop"

- someone who interferes with the natural flow of work

- someone who will report you if you are late or do something wrong

- a person who judges you

- a person who does no work (at least none that you can *see*)

- the "enemy"

- someone who cares more for their own prestige than for your career development

While these images are all too common, they are also symptoms of bad management! Supervision can be positive and helpful, and this is necessary for *successful* work to take place, no matter how large or how small the organization.

SUCCESSFUL SUPERVISION

Successful work can be defined as work that achieves the maximum in positive results while meeting the needs of those doing the work. The four basic needs which everyone must meet in order to be successful as a person and a worker, are:

Belonging—a sense of teamwork

Achievement—challenge and ways to meet it

Fun—enjoyment during work and learning

Freedom—to make choices, have control over important aspects of the work

Too much work in service organizations is not need-fulfilling and, consequently, not successful—it achieves *minimum* positive results with *maximum* stress and anxiety for those doing it. But successful work will be achieved if there is successful supervision.

An achievement-style supervisor, one who embodies the principles of successful management, does the following:

1. Helps, doesn't boss people around.

2. Teaches, doesn't do the work.

3. Is a hard working model.

4. Uses the "YES" Method of Management.

5. Gives each worker individual time.

Supervisors who incorporate these five principles into a supervision style that works for them are successful.

1. HELPS, DOESN'T BOSS PEOPLE AROUND

In every style of organization, the supervisor is responsible for the results of the people s/he supervises. If the staff member you are supervising fails to perform, it is because you did not exercise the principles and practices of good supervision or, when these did not work, you did not fire the person.

A supervisor is therefore required to help the worker to become more successful. It is up to you as supervisor to find the way to help each person to do her/his job better. If you can't help the person, then it is up to you to see that s/he is moved to another position, possibly outside your organization, where s/he can achieve good results.

A supervisor is accountable for all the people "under" her/him. This is not a matter of *blame*, it is a matter of *responsibility*. You are responsible for the morale and effectiveness of the people you supervise.

2. TEACHES, DOESN'T DO THE WORK

Most people get promoted to supervisory positions because they performed their former job well. For example, a successful counselor may be "promoted" to become a supervisor of several other counselors. This promotion is sometimes a mistake. It is much easier to do a job than it is to supervise someone else doing it. How many times have you heard a supervisor say, "Oh, here, let me do it. It'll take less time if I do it than if I explain it to you"?

A good supervisor is actually a teacher. Teaching requires a different set of skills than counseling, for example. When a person is promoted from "worker" to "supervisor," the person doing the promoting rarely says, "Now you will be a teacher and that is a whole new set of skills. You must stop doing the work and start trying to figure out how to help others do it successfully."

Successful teaching involves helping people to meet their basic needs. This requires, first of all, that the supervisor can meet her/his own basic needs successfully and, secondly, that s/he can create a climate in which the workers *help each other* to meet their basic needs. The supervisor can't do all of the helping and should not even try. Promoting a learning atmosphere is the basis of the supervisor's success as a teacher.

Many supervisors continue to do their former work, clinging to it like a security blanket, unable to give it up for the greater responsibility of supervision. If you become aware that you are in a supervisory role but are continuing to do your former work, make the choice. Try to learn supervisory skills. If you don't like it and are not successful at supervising, make the positive choice to resume your former work. Don't look at it as "going back." Look at it as exercising your preference, which is the way you will be most successful in life.

3. IS A HARD WORKING MODEL

Many supervisors believe that their job is to order people around. This is not an effective way to supervise. Effective supervision demands that the supervisor put in hard and visible work *doing supervision.*

The supervisor normally works harder than anyone else. But, beware!

Over-conscientious supervisors can discourage workers by making them feel that no amount of productivity is "enough." If your staff puts in 60 hours of work and then you say to them, "O.K., the next thing for you to do is...," without acknowledging the last 20 hours of overtime, then you are pushing it. Sometimes your staff may tolerate this behavior, knowing that you yourself have just put in even more time, but not indefinitely.

It will contribute to a worker's productivity to have a model supervisor who is a hard worker to imitate. However, the supervisor needs to have reasonable expectations of worker productivity, and the worker needs recognition of her/his efforts and achievements.

4. USES THE "YES" METHOD OF MANAGEMENT

If you look at two organizations—one with a cloud of gloom hovering over it and the other of sunnier mood—what do you think makes the difference? Do you think the gloomy one has less money, more problems? Probably. But those are the end results of an attitude and style of supervision.

If you examine the supervisors in the sunny organization, you will find that they normally say "Yes" when a worker asks for anything—that is, unless the request would be out-and-out destructive! Saying "yes" is so important because this encourages staff to take responsibility for the consequences of their decisions. It helps people to exercise their decision-making skills.

If the supervisor says "Yes," then the worker must try to make the requested idea work successfully. If it does, it is an achievement (thus meeting a basic need). If it does not, the worker still has exercised her/his basic need for decision-making freedom and will take the consequences of the decision. Note that the consequences should suit the risk. A person should not be blamed nor punished, but held accountable. "When can you do it?" "Is it still a good idea?"

The supervisor should try to say "Yes" as much as possible, but if the request would hurt someone or the organization, the supervisor should say "No" and mean it.

Try to make saying "Yes" a habit.

5. GIVES EACH WORKER INDIVIDUAL TIME

While this principle is listed last, it may be the most important of all five principles.

It can be safely stated that if a supervisor does not have time to give each person s/he is supervising at least 45 minutes per week of uninterrupted time, privately, then the supervisor is overseeing too many people and/or is over-extended. *There is no replacement for this quality time.* Supervisors have a multitude of excuses why they do not have time to do individual supervision once a week. If the supervisor does not have time for individual supervision, then s/he is probably doing too much of the staff's work. Frequently this is because the supervisor feels competent at doing that work, but not at doing the new work of supervising. The job of a supervisor is to supervise—not to do the staff's work. By using the methods outlined here, this can cease to be a problem.

WHAT TO DO IN INDIVIDUAL SUPERVISION

1. Each session should begin with some informal "involvement time." An easy way to do this is for each person to share the highlights of what's happening with her/himself both personally and professionally.

2. In the next part of the session the staff member should be asked to describe at least one positive accomplishment since the last session and one thing the staff member had problems with. The supervisor also should tell about one thing the staff member did well and some area that may need improvement. This works best if both people have thought about these things in advance, *written* them down, and come to the supervisory session prepared to discuss them.

3. The staff member should be asked to pick one thing to work on in the coming week and before leaving the session he should have a specific plan to do it.

4. The staff member then should be given ample opportunity to ask questions or bring up other issues.

5. The *last* thing to do is to handle any administrative details or procedures. Note, this is the first thing that most supervisors do—but save it for the end of the session.

COMPLAINTS

One of the problems in individual supervision is that staff members tend to use this time to complain, but a skillful supervisor can turn this negative situation into a positive one. Complaining has two purposes. One is to get the recipient of the complaint mobilized to assist the complainer in getting what s/he wants. The second is to reduce tension through ventilation of frustration. The ultimate goal of the supervisor is to assist the complainer to evaluate what s/he is presently doing and then problem-solving to choose new behaviors to get what s/he needs.

Format for handling complaints:

"How would you like it to be?"

"What have you been doing to get what you say you want?"

"Is what you've been doing working?"

"Would you like to figure out another way to get what you want?"

When a person complains, the supervisor needs to listen just long enough to get a rough idea what the situation is (two or three sentences). A complaint is different from a request for a change in that a complaint has an urgent emotional component, and the message conveys what the person does not want rather than what s/he does want.

As soon as the complainer stops for a breath, the supervisor needs to ask, "How would you like it to be?" This question should pull the "do want" out of the "don't want". Often the complainer will restate the "don't want" with increased fervor. The supervisor can then say simply, "I understand you're upset, and I want to help you," this statement being gauged to reduce frustration, and then again search out the ideal picture, "If things were working the way you want them to, what would be happening?" If the "do want" is still not forthcoming, make one more attempt, "You're telling me what you *don't* want. I need to know what you *do* want."

When the supervisor gets a clear picture of what the staff member wants to happen, s/he then asks, "What have you been doing to get what you say you want?" When an answer is given, the supervisor then asks the staff member to evaluate how effective her/his behavior has been by asking, "How's that been working for you?" Here is an example of how such a session might progress:

STAFF: I'm sick and tired of being changed from shift to shift and never knowing which center I'm working in or with whom. The shift supervisor never asks me ahead of time.

MANAGER: How would you like it to be?

STAFF: I'd like him to quit treating me like I'm a mindless commodity.

MANAGER: How would you like him to treat you? What do you want to hear from him?

STAFF: I'd like him to say, "I need your help in figuring this out, John."

MANAGER: What have you been doing to get what you want?

STAFF: --silence--

MANAGER: Who have you been talking to? What have you been thinking?

STAFF: I've been keeping it to myself, but I've been thinking "Screw this job," and slacking off.

MANAGER: How's that been working for you?

STAFF: --pause-- It hasn't.

MANAGER: Do you want to figure out a better way to handle it?

STAFF: Yes, can you help me?

MANAGER: Sure, I have some ideas.

The question, "Do you want to figure out a better way?", is asking for a decision to plan. If in the opinion of the supervisor the situation is not within the control of the manager or staff, then the appropriate question here would be, "Would it be helpful if you could figure out another way to look at this situation?"

Sometimes the complaint is not within control of the complainer, such as complaints about the weather, immutable policies, or past events. In this case, it is helpful if the supervisor asks the person to assess the situation with the simple question, "Is the change you wish within your control?" If the answer to this question is "No," the supervisor needs to ask the complainer, "Is choosing to worry about things you cannot change a good use of your energy, or would it be better to look at some areas where you can have some impact?"

If the staff member resists an offer to plan, the supervisor can then offer a third alternative which would be, "Do you just want to complain?" (smile) or "Do you just need to get this off your chest?" If an affirmative response is received, the supervisor then needs to indicate a time limit. "O.K., I've got two minutes (smile)," or "O.K., I've got ten minutes, go for it." The supervisor may then choose to play a more active role, encouraging the complaint by saying, "And further more!"..."And what else!"..."How bad!"..."Spit it out!"...(almost as though a cheering section). This approach speeds up the ventilation by quickly exhausting the complainer. From my experience, the ventilator can only sustain the complaint for 3-5 minutes if the manager behaves in this fashion. Limiting the time for complaining lets the staff member know that the supervisor who has plenty of time to solve problems does not lend much of her/his valuable time to complaints. S/he can even explain this, if questioned, by saying that listening to complaints is an energy drain on her/his and doesn't lead to solutions. Solutions only come through planned action or change of perspective. A skilled supervisor will also develop the expectation with her/his staff that if staff members want to present her/his with a problem they must also bring with them a couple possible solutions for consideration.

Humor can play a role in defusing chronic complaints, but only if it fits the personality of the supervisor, if the complaint is not serious, or if the complaint is one that is frequently repeated. Inherent in the humor can be subtle learning for the complainer who has the choice to receive it or not. Also, laughter is effective in reducing frustration.

A supervisor can use the game "Complain To Me" during staff in-service training to introduce the concept of switching a negative complaint into a positive want. The game is basically a role play with two people—one the complainer and one the complaint recipient. The idea is to practice the appropriate questions that turn the complaint from "don't want" to "do want" to problem solving. To start the game "Complain To Me" the supervisor should model it for the group with a volunteer, then pair up individuals to "complain" to each other. This activity can be done while walking, which is so often the case in real life. Partners can be switched every 5 minutes. This is an involving, fun activity after which no staff member can ever again quite so effectively complain. There will be immediate application to the work setting as the question "How would you like it to be?" echoes through the staff room.

HOW MANY PEOPLE SHOULD A SUPERVISOR SUPERVISE?

What is the ideal ratio of supervisors to workers? While there are obviously many exceptions, my experience has shown that each supervisor can usually *successfully* supervise four or five people. Some of the variables involved in the number of workers a supervisor can handle effectively are:

1. The supervisor's experience: an experienced supervisor will be able to handle more workers than the first-time supervisor.

2. The range or variety of the workers' work: when all the workers in a group are doing very similar jobs, a larger number of workers can be supervised by one person than when the individuals are all doing very different jobs.

3. The complexity of the work being supervised: typists' work, for example, would be less complicated to supervise than a team of people who are, in turn, supervising others.

HOW MANY PEOPLE DO *YOU* SUPERVISE?

Do you know how many people you supervise? Ask others in your organization what they think. You may be surprised at the discrepancy between your opinions. In one organization, at the beginning of a staff development project, a supervisor was asked how many people he supervised. He said, "Two." A survey of the other 30 staff revealed that 18 people thought this person was their supervisor! This is an extreme example, but less extreme versions of it are common.

Be sure your organization has a clear supervisory structure. Supervisors must know *exactly* whom they are supervising!

HELPFUL BOOKS ON SUPERVISION

CONTROL THEORY by Dr. William Glasser, M.D. This is an explanation for laymen of Control Theory, the theory behind Reality Therapy. It is a very clear and convincing explanation of basic psychological needs and how these affect behavior.

THE ONE-MINUTE MANAGER by Kenneth Blanchard and Spencer Johnson. This small book has the basic message of giving immediate feedback, both good and not so good. This increases worker productivity and saves wear and tear on the supervisor. It comes close to embodying the five principles recommended here for supervision and shows how people meet their needs in the workplace without describing it in those words.

V. STAFF MEETINGS

Most supervisors spend (and waste) a lot of time in meetings. Obviously, if your meetings can be streamlined, you will have more time for other supervisory tasks – or for yourself!

In order for meetings to be productive they should be need-fulfilling for all the people involved in the meeting—including you. A meeting which drags on and on when staff members have work to do, clients to see, etc., is the opposite of need-fulfilling. When staff members are required to attend meetings, and then are not asked for input, the meetings are not need-fulfilling.

If your meeting has been need-fulfilling, staff members will leave the meeting:

- having a sense of belonging to the staff (LOVE)

- knowing that their opinions were listened to and valued (POWER)

- having had a few laughs (FUN)

- having had some choices about what was happening both in the meeting and in the organization (FREEDOM)

Learning how to run a meeting that is short, to the point and satisfying is not difficult. The difficult part is *using* the knowledge *each time* you meet. It's difficult to stay disciplined, but in this case discipline pays off. Your staff will be happier and so will you. Meetings can become a pleasure, not a pain.

WHAT HAPPENS IN A *GOOD* MEETING?

There are four important success factors the supervisor must consider: (1) Environment & Logistics, (2) Purpose, (3) Agenda, (4) Participation.

1. ENVIRONMENT & LOGISTICS

    (a) Secure the best meeting room your organization has to offer. If there is a table in the middle, have it removed if possible. Arrange the number of chairs you need in a circle or semi-circle.

    (b) Announce before the meeting how much time the meeting will take. A meeting longer than 90 minutes generally becomes counter-productive. Shorter is better. This takes practice, but as you develop a format for your meetings and some discipline in the meetings, you will be able to gauge the time factor successfully.

    (c) Have an easel and flip chart in the room. Remember to bring a marking pen and masking tape to put up pages you have used but want to continue to see. Ask for a volunteer (you can rotate this person) to write for the group on the flip chart. Writing down key points of the discussion as the meeting progresses lets people know they have been heard. Number all the pieces of chart paper in order. At the end of the meeting give them to the Secretary. The chart pages from one meeting should be brought to the next meeting, but then can be destroyed–they do not take the place of minutes.

    (d) Always start with an involvement activity of some sort. See the chapter on Personal Involvement for suggestions.

    (e) Review the last meeting by discussing it or reading the minutes. While this takes time, it also saves a lot of time by preventing re-making decisions.

2. PURPOSE

Before the meeting, let the people attending the meeting know the purpose of the meeting. This also *defines* the purpose of the meeting for you. Clarify your own meeting situation on the following checklist.

What is the Purpose of Your Staff Meeting?

Planning: Discussing work to be done.

Problem Solving: Resolving an issue.

Training: Explaining work to be done.

Strategy: Figuring out how to do something.

Information Exchange: Talking about what happened.

Planning: Deciding what to do.

3. AGENDA

   (a) Building an agenda

   Some supervisors come to a meeting with the
   agenda already typed up. This does not
   encourage group participation. Ask staff to bring
   agenda items to the meeting. Start with theirs,
   then add yours. It is more participatory to build
   the agenda at the outset of the meeting. Have the
   group prioritize agenda items in order of
   importance.

   (b) Allocate time for agenda items

   Once the agenda items have been prioritized,
   decide how much time you will spend on each
   item depending on the length of the meeting.
   STICK TO IT! NO MATTER WHAT!   Have a
   group member volunteer to be the timer. Each
   agenda item should be written on the chart paper
   with a time beside it. Five minutes before time is
   up the timer should announce to the group that it
   is time for closure. Try to select a strict timer.
   This is a great job for your *least* flexible staff
   member!

   (c) Minutes

   Tracking the group's decisions, reports and plans
   will provide for the measurement of progress and
   accomplishment necessary to meet participants'
   psychological needs and give the organization
   accountability. The important records to keep
   are:

   • reports (which can be typed and photocopied
     before the meeting, then attached to minutes of
     the meeting)

   • votes or final decisions

   • plans (which can be taken from the chart pages
     and typed up later by the secretary)

60

4. PARTICIPATION

(a) Start each meeting with a short involvement activity.

(b) There are more creative ways to run a meeting than to have all of the staff sitting around taking turns talking. Frequently, the meeting would be more productive if the group were divided into teams who report later to the whole group. This approach is also less boring. When you divide the group and give each group a task in which all members can participate, the meeting becomes need-fulfilling for all involved. In most meetings, the vocal people talk, the quieter ones sit back and say very little even though they might have a lot to contribute. Dividing into small groups can prevent this.

SUMMARY

Use the following meeting format. Write it on a piece of chart paper and post it in your meeting area to use as a guide.

1. Involvement Activity

2. Review last meeting

3. Create agenda or add to it

4. Reports

5. Problem solving and decisions; formal vote if necessary

6. Summary of meeting (optional)

This is a brief guide to better meetings. You *can* have better meetings if you *want* to have better meetings. Do some reading, studying and practicing. The meetings will get better and you will have more time.

HELPFUL BOOKS ON MEETINGS

HOW TO MAKE MEETINGS WORK—THE INTERACTION METHOD by David Straus and Michael Doyle, published by Wyden Books (hardback) and Playboy Press (paperback). If your organization can only afford to buy one book to improve its management, buy this one. It is a practical, easy-to-learn approach to new meeting styles, much of the technology for them having been developed by these two. The only important aspect not covered by this book is structured involvement activities, although the process itself is involving.

TAKING PART, by Lawrence Halprin and Jim Burns, published by MIT Press, Cambridge, Massachusetts. This book is also a practical how-to manual on meetings, facilitation and the group planning process. The authors have involved large numbers of people in planning their community environments.

VI. STAFF EVALUATION

The only *effective* evaluation is that which helps people meet their basic psychological needs at work. It is presumed that evaluation is being done to increase productivity and to increase accountability within the organization. Productivity can be measured when there are work goals being achieved by individuals. Accountability is keeping track of what people are doing. Both of these areas are affected by evaluation. Setting work goals and tracking work in relation to the goals dramatically improves not only the work but the worker's attitude towards it.

The four basic psychological needs which are met through positive evaluation are:

Belonging: Evaluation implies the worker is an important part of the organization. Belonging is enhanced when the goals of the individual's work are related to the goals of the organization. Team effort is established through understanding one's role within the organization.

Achievement: This need is partially met when the goals which were established with and for the worker are met and acknowledged. These measurable successes are the key to the worker's individual growth as well as the organization's productivity.

Fun: While anticipating an evaluation may cause anxiety in the worker, or even the supervisor, the process ought to be structured as pleasantly as possible. The less formal the environment, the more likely the outcome will be successful.

Freedom to decide: If the evaluation is set up with the supervisor and the worker sharing equal responsibility for ideas, both will meet their need for autonomy.

TWO EVALUATION METHODS

The two personnel evaluation methods I present here are based on meeting these four basic needs. Therefore, they can help the staff to succeed, to improve themselves, to change a job role or pay level. The evaluation methods may reveal the need for firing someone, although that is a last resort and unlikely if good evaluation and management methods are being used.

These two evaluation methods, The Ideal Game and the Performance Appraisal Packet, are both based on the worker being able to evaluate her/himself before the supervisor does. Also, the worker begins by identifying her/his strengths before going on to areas that need improvement. It is not useful to call areas to be improved "weaknesses," because weakness implies that nothing can be done about it. "Areas to be improved" is a positive definition that shows there is hope. Self-evaluation, with positive attributes and accomplish- ments being considered first, meets the worker's basic needs better than a typical critical evaluation by a supervisor, which is why it is more effective. The needs for belonging, achievement, fun, and freedom are shortchanged when a worker is expected to be a passive listener to a list of negative criticisms.

The Ideal Game is an informal way to work with an entire group of staff members. It can be the basis of cohesive teamwork, solve staff problems, and the ideas generated by the game can be used in individual supervision sessions. The Performance Appraisal Packet is a more formal method of evaluation. It should be used once a year with each staff member.

THE IDEAL GAME

A. OVERVIEW

1. WHEN TO DO IT

If the supervisor has not been doing individual supervision, the Ideal Game is a good way to start. Otherwise it should be done about twice a year. You can tell it's needed when a lot of semi-hidden, petty grievances seem to be floating around and morale is low. The Ideal Game provides a positive environment to solve problems and lift spirits.

2. WHO IS INVOLVED?

Anyone in a working group in the organization can participate. It will work with as few as two people. There is no upper limit, but if the group is very large the process takes too long. Unless the unity of a large group is at stake, divide into sub-groups of no more than six.

3. SET UP

If the groups have six people, set aside about two hours for the Ideal Game. Smaller groups will take less time, larger groups take longer. Add about 20 minutes for each person over six if you must do it in a larger group.

Set up chairs in a semicircle. Tape *lots* of chart paper on the wall at the front of the semicircle. Arrange for there to be no calls or interruptions.

It is especially good if you start the Ideal Game with a short involvement activity. If the goal of your meeting is team building, the involvement activity can be as much as an hour and a half long. If the goal of your meeting is evaluation, a 5-10 minute involvement activity will do.

4. WHY IT WORKS SO WELL

Most people are their own biggest critic. If you have a complaint about someone, usually the person is already aware of the problem. When a positive climate is offered, the average person welcomes the opportunity to unburden her/himself. During the Ideal Game, staff members are often amazed to see "problem" staff members clearly identify their own problems. This allows more open communication among staff members.

B. STEPS TO DO THE IDEAL GAME

1. BRAINSTORM

One person acts as both recorder and facilitator, or two people can lead, one for each role.

The facilitator asks everyone to call out *every* quality s/he can think of for the Ideal Staff Person to have. As people brainstorm the qualities, the recorder writes them on the chart paper with wide-tipped felt markers. The qualities most often named are things like cheerful, on time, good looking, rich, etc. Jokes are encouraged. This helps make the activity more enjoyable. As many qualities as possible are generated. If someone calls out a negative quality like "never late," the facilitator helps think of the positive or "ideal" side of it, such as "always on time." The recorder writes everything *except* the negatives.

2. PICKING QUALITIES FOR ONESELF

After all the qualities everyone can think of have
been listed, the facilitator explains that each person
will pick from the list 4 or 5 qualities that s/he thinks
s/he has and write them down. Then each person
picks from the list two things s/he would like to
improve about her/himself. The group needs a few
minutes to do this in silence.

3. SHARING THE LISTS

In order to provide a model for others the facilitator
goes first. S/he will say, "Some qualities I think I
have are...," and after sharing her/his list will ask,
"What other qualities on the list do you think I
have?" The group will add several things. This is an
essential part of the exercise because it provides a
safety net for the next part which is areas that need
improvement.

The facilitator then says, "Some things I would
like to improve are....," and names the two qualities
s/he wrote down. Members of the group may
mention additional areas they see needing
improvement and should consider whether these are
related to what the person has already identified. It
will help the person receiving the feedback if it is tied
to the qualities s/he mentioned himself.

After the facilitator, each person in the group has a
turn using the same format.

4. PLANNING FOR IMPROVEMENT

At this point several courses can be followed.

(a) The facilitator and members of the group can take turns helping each other plan how to improve one area.

(b) The group can divide into pairs with each pair helping each other to make a plan.

(c) The group can wait until a one-to-one supervision session and work out a plan at that time.

A good plan needs to be specific, do-able, and enacted in the immediate future. When, for example, a person who wants to improve punctuality says, "I plan to be on time from now on," the facilitator should keep asking for specifics until the plan sounds more like, "I plan to be on time tomorrow by setting my alarm clock a half hour earlier."

A buddy system will help to be sure plans are followed and will take some of the supervisory pressure off the group leader. While people are planning, the facilitator should ask, "How can someone else help you with that?" Plans involving two people are better than plans done alone. Or, after the plan is finished, the facilitator can ask each person at the end of their turn, "Who would you like to be your buddy to help you or to report to?" This way each person identifies his own "buddy" to work with.

PERFORMANCE APPRAISAL PACKET

A. OVERVIEW

1. WHAT IS IT?

The Performance Appraisal Packet is a 5-page system designed to evaluate how well a person is doing his job. In this activity "performance" means what the person does on the job, "appraisal" means how well the person is doing the job.

2. WHO DOES IT?

The method is used by two people, the evaluator (supervisor) and the person being evaluated. Both have active roles in the process. It begins with self-evaluation by the staff member and includes evaluation by the supervisor.

3. WHEN IT IS DONE?

At least once a year every individual in every working group in an organization should routinely participate in this evaluation method. If the organization is changing fast, an individual is having problems on the job, or when you need to consider raises, bonuses, promotions, etc., the method can be used more often.

4. WHAT WILL IT DO FOR YOU?

The Performance Appraisal Packet provides a positive method for evaluating staff. This method also builds morale, identifies training needs, and clarifies expectations for each person's role in the organization.

B. HOW TO USE THE PERFORMANCE APPRAISAL PACKET

1. PREPARE

Type the pages as indicated on the following pages. Photocopy them so they can be used over and over by many evaluators/people being evaluated.

2. FIRST MEETING

The evaluator will meet with the person to be evaluated and explain how the packet is to be used. The supervisor and the person being evaluated fill out the pages after this meeting, privately. The supervisor fills out the packet regarding the person to be evaluated, and the person being evaluated fills out the packet as a self-evaluation.

3. EVALUATION MEETING

The supervisor and person being evaluated get together to discuss the packet. The person being evaluated *always* goes first. Then, during the same step, the supervisor gives her/his opinion. (Note to the supervisor: Start the meeting with a short involvement activity.)

When discussing Page 4 of the packet, the supervisor should try to think of a dozen or more accomplishments. They must be specific. Not, "Nice work," but "Your typing speed has improved more than 20%!" or "I saw you being helpful to the sick lady who was in here the other day." Refer to actual incidents as much as possible. Give examples. Elaborate. This is part of the person's "reward for service."

WHAT THE PERFORMANCE APPRAISAL PACKET LOOKS LIKE

Use regular typing paper to make up each of these pages:

PAGE 1

Name of Person:

Note to person being evaluated: Don't mind your writing style, spelling or grammar. Just write so you can read it.

LIST all the work items you have done in two days. Pick any two days. Add more paper if you need to.

PAGE 2

Using the information from Page 1, group the activities into 4 or 5 categories that seem to be similar. Try to estimate the time you spent on each category.

PAGE 3

Give each category from Page 2 a title. Number the titles, 1 through 5 or whatever number, in order of time spent (least to most).

Give one or two goals for each Activity. A "goal" means, why are you doing it? What good will it do?

PAGE 4

Describe <u>three</u> accomplishments since the last evaluation, or in the past year. Add paper if you like. Be
ready to give some examples of each accomplishment.

Describe one thing you would like to improve about
your own performance.

Describe one thing you would <u>like help from someone
else</u> to improve about your own performance. If you
want to name the helper or helpers you'd like, go ahead.

Describe one change in the organization which would
help you do a better job.

Use regular typing paper to make up this page. This is a sample list. An evaluator should make up her/his own list including appropriate items from the list below and any other items specific to her/his organization. Double space your list.

PAGE 5

EVALUATION CHECKLIST

Check off your opinion in the appropriate column.

Work Area	Out- standing	Satis- factory	Minor Imprvmt Needed	Major Imprvmt Needed	Does Not Apply
Creative problem solving					
Working with others					
Working independently					
Organizing work effectively					
Writing effectively					
Oral communication					
Adapting to new assignments					
Technical knowledge/skills					
Finishing things					
Knowing/applying organization policies					
Preparing reports					
Co-operation					
Reliability					
Training others					
Motivating others					
Delegating duties/authority					
Openness to learning					
Courtesy to public					
Rapport with public					
Addressing client needs					
Ability to listen					
Helpfulness					
Punctuality					
Productivity					
Quality of work					
Accuracy/attention to detail					
Performance under pressure					

CONCLUSION

If, as the boss or supervisor, you have tried all the methods here and have not been able to help an employee do an adequate job, meet her/his needs, or the needs of the organization, it is time to do what primarily has given bosses a bad name—get rid of the employee (fire him!). If you have used the methods in this book (especially the Performance Appraisal Packet), you will have evidence that the person has not been doing her/his job. *Never* fire a person without *written* documentation. Most agencies and organizations have a policy about this. Be sure to find out what the procedure is.

When you make the hard decision that a person must go, try telling the person in such a way that you communicate the idea, "You are in the wrong job." Be sure to ask the person if s/he is happy in the job. About 95% of the time the answer will be, "No." *Help* the person to think of jobs s/he would be happy in. Be a personal friend, but remember your role involvement. Your job is to be sure the organization runs efficiently. Firing an employee is hard, but allowing an unproductive employee to demoralize the rest of the staff will work against what you are working for—a need-fulfilling organization.